•••◉ *BULLETPOINTS* ◉•••

UNIVERSE

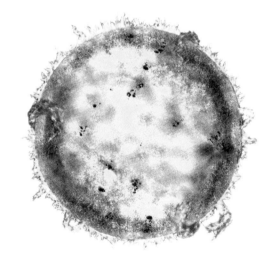

John Farndon
Consultant: Tim Furniss

Miles Kelly
PUBLISHING

First published in 2004 by Miles Kelly Publishing Ltd
Bardfield Centre, Great Bardfield
Essex, CM7 4SL

Some material in this book first appeared in *1000 Things You Should Know*

2 4 6 8 10 9 7 5 3 1

Editor: Belinda Gallagher

Assistant Editor: Mark Darling

Picture Research: Liberty Newton

Production: Estela Godoy

British Library Cataloguing-in-Publication Data
A catalogue record for this book is available from the British Library

ISBN 1-84236-377-8

Printed in China

www.mileskelly.net
info@mileskelly.net

The publishers would like to thank the following artists who have contributed to this book:
Julie Banyard, Kuo Kang Chen, Nick Farmer, Mike Foster/Maltings, Alan Hancocks, Robert Holder, Rob Jakeway, Janos
Marffy, Martin Sanders, Peter Sarson, Guy Smith, Sarah Smith, Rudi Vizi, Paul Williams, John Woodcock

The publishers would also like to thank the following source for the use of their photograph:
Page 38 Leif Skoogfors

Contents

The Universe

- **The Universe is everything** that we can ever know – all of space and all of time.

- **The Universe is almost entirely empty**, with small clusters of matter and energy.

- **The Universe is probably** about 15 billion years old, but estimates vary.

- **One problem with working out** the age of the Universe is that there are stars in our galaxy which are thought to be 14 to 18 billion years old – older than the estimated age of the Universe. So either the stars must be younger, or the Universe older.

- **The furthest galaxies yet detected** are about 13 billion light-years away (130 billion trillion km).

- **The Universe is getting bigger** by the second. We know this because all the galaxies are zooming away from us. The further away they are, the faster they are moving.

- **The very furthest galaxies** are spreading away from us at more than 90% of the speed of light.

- **The Universe was once thought** to be everything that could ever exist, but recent theories about inflation (see the Big Bang) suggest our Universe may be just one of countless bubbles of space-time.

- **The Universe may have neither** a centre nor an edge, because according to Einstein's theory of relativity (see Einstein), gravity bends all of space-time around into an endless curve.

▲ *The Universe is getting bigger and bigger all the time, as galaxies rush outwards in all directions.*

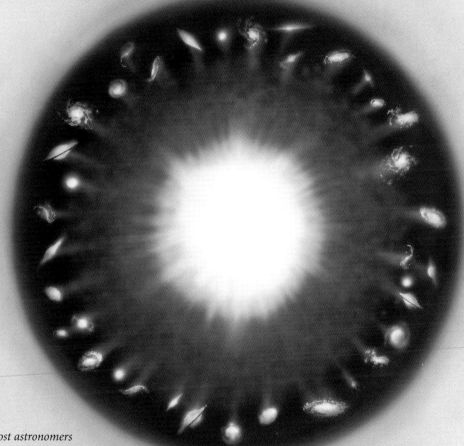

▲ *Most astronomers
believe that the Universe
was created in a huge explosion
called 'the Big Bang', seen here as a flash in the
middle of the image. It occurred in just a fraction of a
second, and sent matter flying out in all directions.*

. . . . . **FASCINATING FACT** . . . . .
Recent theories suggest there may
be many other universes which we can
never know.

The Big Bang

- **The Big Bang explosion** is how scientists think the Universe began some 15 billion years ago.

- **First there was a hot ball** tinier than an atom. This cooled to 10 billion billion °C as it grew to football size.

- **A split second later,** a super-force swelled the infant Universe a thousand billion billion billion times. Scientists call this inflation.

- **As it mushroomed out,** the Universe was flooded with energy and matter, and the super-force separated into basic forces such as electricity and gravity.

- **There were no atoms at first,** just tiny particles such as quarks in a dense soup a trillion trillion trillion trillion trillion times denser than water.

- **There was also antimatter,** the mirror image of matter. Antimatter and matter destroy each other when they meet, so they battled it out. Matter just won – but the Universe was left almost empty.

- **After three minutes,** quarks started to fuse (join) to make the smallest atoms, hydrogen. Then hydrogen gas atoms fused to make helium gas atoms.

- **After one million years** the gases began to curdle into strands with dark holes between them.

- **After 300 million years,** the strands clumped into clouds, and then the clouds clumped together to form stars and galaxies.

- **The afterglow of the Big Bang** can still be detected as microwave background radiation coming from all over space (see picture above).

▼ *Before the Big Bang all the material that existed was contained in one small lump. The material was forced out causing the Universe to expand rapidly. The galaxies are still moving away from one another and some scientists believe that they will continue to move apart forever.*

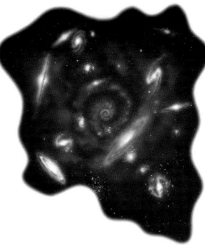

◀ *The millions of stars that are visible in the night sky are still just a tiny part of the Universe.*

▼ *The Big Bang was a massive explosion that created the Universe.*

▶ *Millions of years later, gases clustered into clouds.*

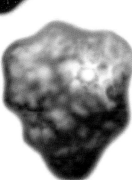

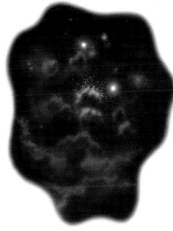

▲ *The clouds formed together to form galaxies.*

7

Extraterrestrials

- **Extraterrestrial (ET)** means 'outside the Earth'.

- **Some scientists** say that ET life could develop anywhere in the Universe where there is a flow of energy.

- **One extreme idea** is that space clouds could become sentient (thinking) beings.

- **Most scientists** believe that if there is ET life anywhere in the Universe, it must be based on the chemistry of carbon, as life on Earth is.

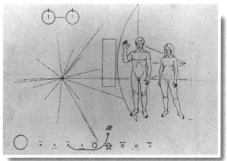

- **If civilizations like ours** exist elsewhere, they may be on planets circling other stars. This is why the discovery of other planetary systems is so exciting (see planets).

▲ *The space probes* Pioneer 10 *and* 11 *carry metal panels with picture messages about life on Earth into deep space.*

- **The Drake Equation** was proposed by astronomer Frank Drake to work out how many civilizations there could be in our galaxy – and the figure is millions!

- **There is no scientific proof** that any ET life form has ever visited the Earth.

- **SETI** is the Search for Extraterrestrial Intelligence – the programme that analyzes radio signals from space for signs of intelligent life.

- **The Arecibo radio telescope** beams out signals to distant stars.

▶ *Many photographs of UFOs (Unidentified Flying Objects) such as this exist. Some people claim that these prove the existence of life and craft elsewhere in the Universe.*

...FASCINATING FACT...
The life chemical formaldehyde can be
detected in radio emissions from the
galaxy NGC 253.

Clusters

- **The Milky Way** belongs to a cluster of 30 galaxies called the Local Group.

- **The Local Group** is seven million light-years across.

- **There are three giant spiral galaxies** in the Local Group, plus 15 ellipticals and 13 irregulars, such as the Large Magellanic Cloud.

- **Beyond the Local Group** are many millions of similar star clusters.

- **The Virgo cluster** is 50 million light-years away and is made up of more than 1000 galaxies.

- **The Local Group plus millions** of other clusters make up a huge group called the Local Supercluster.

- **Other superclusters** are Hercules and Pegasus.

- **Superclusters** are separated by huge voids (empty space), which the superclusters surround like the film around a soap bubble.

- **The voids between superclusters** measure 350 to 400 million light-years across.

> **FASCINATING FACT**
> One film of superclusters makes up a vast structure called the Great Wall. It is the largest structure in the Universe – over 700 million light-years long, but just 30 million thick.

▶ *Space looks like a formless collection of stars and clouds, but all matter tends to cluster together.*

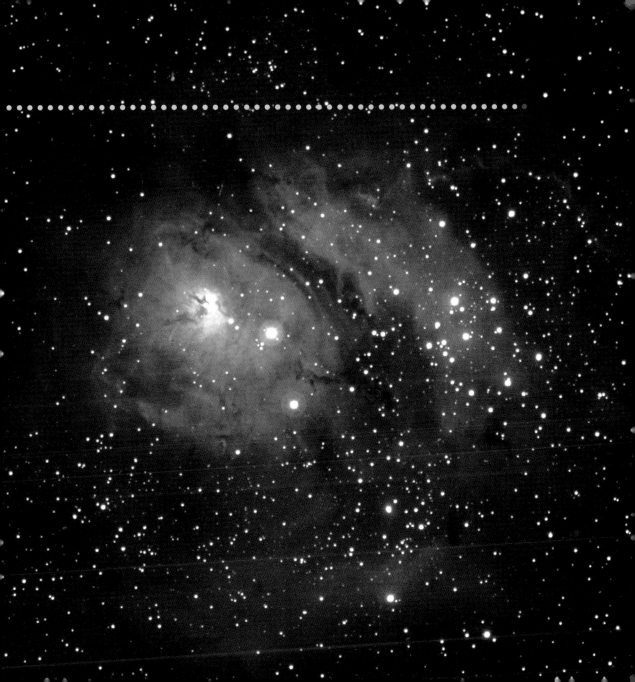

Quasars

- **Quasars** are the most intense sources of light in the Universe. Although no bigger than the Solar System, they glow with the brightness of 100 galaxies.

- **Quasars are the most distant** known objects in the Universe. Even the nearest is billions of light-years away.

- **The most distant quasar** is on the very edges of the known Universe, 12 billion light-years away.

- **Some quasars** are so far away that we see them as they were when the Universe was still in its infancy – 20% of its current age.

- **Quasar** is short for Quasi-Stellar (star-like) Radio Object. This comes from the fact that the first quasars were detected by the strong radio signals they give out, and also because quasars are so small and bright that at first people thought they looked like stars.

- **Only one of the 200 quasars** now known actually beams out radio signals, so the term Quasi-Stellar Radio Object is in fact misleading!

- **The brightest** quasar is 3C 273, two billion light-years away.

- **Quasars** are at the heart of galaxies called 'active galaxies'.

- **Quasars** may get their energy from a black hole at their core, which draws in matter ferociously.

- **The black hole** in a quasar may pull in matter with the same mass as 100 million Suns.

▲ *The Hubble space telescope's clear view of space has given the best-ever photographs of quasars. This is a picture of the quasar PKS2349, billions of light-years away.*

▲ *Quasars are extremely lumious objects at the centre of some distant galaxies. Most quasars are about the size of the Solar System.*

Distances

- **The distance to the Moon** is measured with a laser beam.

- **The distance to the planets** is measured by bouncing radar signals off them and timing how long the signals take to get there and back.

- **The distance to nearby stars** is worked out by measuring the slight shift in the angle of each star in comparison to stars far away, as the Earth orbits the Sun. This is called parallax shift.

- **Parallax shift** can only be used to measure nearby stars, so astronomers work out the distance to faraway stars and galaxies by comparing how bright they look with how bright they actually are.

- **For middle distance stars,** astronomers compare colour with brightness using the Hertzsprung-Russell (H-R) diagram. This is called main sequence fitting.

- **Beyond 30,000 light-years,** stars are too faint for main sequence fitting to work.

- **Distances to nearby galaxies** can be estimated using 'standard candles' – stars whose brightness astronomers know, such as Cepheid variables.

▲ *Estimating the distance to the stars is one of the major problems in astronomy.*

- **The expected brightness of a galaxy** too far away to pick out its stars may be worked out using the Tully-Fisher technique, based on how fast galaxies spin.

- **Counting planetary nebulae** (the rings of gas left behind by supernova explosions) is another way of working out how bright a distant galaxy should be.

- **A third method** of calculating the brightness of a distant galaxy is to gauge how mottled it looks.

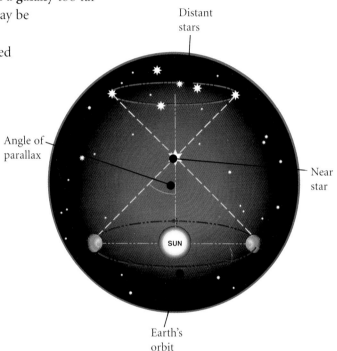

Distant stars

Angle of parallax

Near star

SUN

Earth's orbit

▲ *Parallax is the apparent movement of a nearby star against the background of more distant stars, not caused by the movement of the star itself, but by the Earth's motion.*

15

Einstein

- **The great scientist Albert Einstein** (1879-1955) is most famous for creating the two theories of relativity.

- **Special relativity** (1905) shows that all measurements are relative, including time and speed. In other words, time and speed depend on where you measure them.

- **The fastest thing in the Universe,** light, is the same speed everywhere and always passes at the same speed – no matter where you are or how fast you are going.

- **Special relativity** shows that as things travel faster, they seem to shrink in length and get heavier. Their time stretches too – that is, their clocks seem to run slower.

- **The theory of general relativity** (1915) includes the idea of special relativity, but also shows how gravity works.

- **General relativity** shows that gravity's pull is acceleration (speed) – gravity and acceleration are the same.

- **When things are falling** their acceleration cancels out gravity, which is why astronauts in orbit are weightless.

- **If gravity and acceleration** are the same, gravity must bend light rays simply by stretching space (and time).

- **Gravity works by bending space** (and time). 'Matter tells space how to bend; space tells matter how to move.'

- **General relativity** predicts that light rays from distant stars will be bent by the gravitational pull of stars they pass.

▲▶ *Einstein's theory of general relativity was proved right in 1919, when light rays from a distant star just grazing the Sun were measured during an eclipse and shown to be slightly bent.*

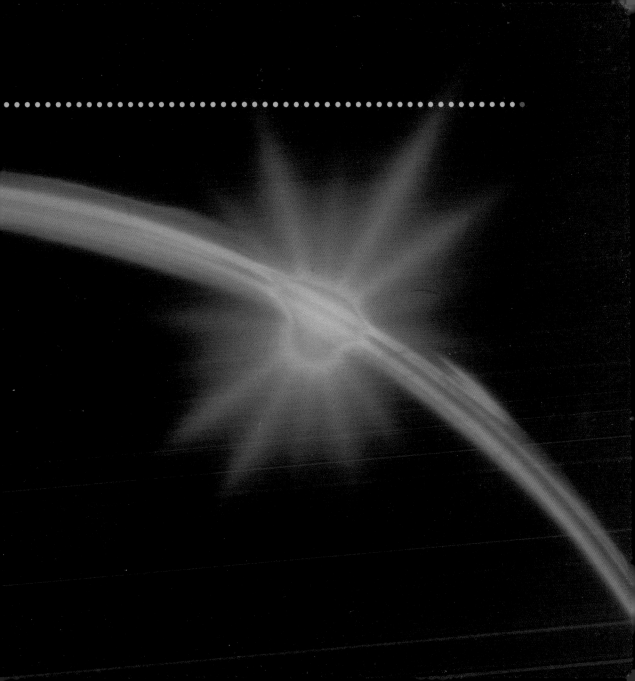

Atoms

- **Atoms are the building blocks** of the Universe, the invisibly small particles from which matter is made.

- **Atoms are so small** that you could fit a billion on the full stop at the end of this sentence.

- **Atoms** are the very smallest identifiable piece of a chemical element (see elements).

- **There are** as many different atoms as elements.

- **Atoms are mostly empty space** dotted with tiny sub-atomic particles (subatomic is 'smaller than an atom').

- **The core of an atom** is a nucleus made of a cluster of two kinds of subatomic particle – protons and neutrons.

- **Whizzing around the nucleus** are even tinier particles called electrons.

- **Electrons have** a negative electrical charge, and protons have a positive charge, so electrons are held to the nucleus by electrical attraction.

- **Under certain conditions** atoms can be split into over 200 kinds of short-lived subatomic particle. The particles of the nucleus are made from various even tinier particles called quarks.

▶ *This diagram cannot show the buzzing cloud of energy that is a real atom! Electrons (blue) whizz around the nucleus, made of protons (red) and neutrons (green).*

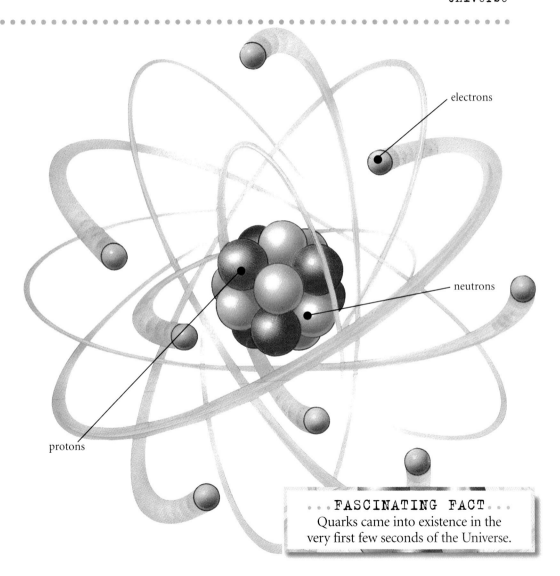

electrons

neutrons

protons

...FASCINATING FACT...
Quarks came into existence in the
very first few seconds of the Universe.

Nuclear energy

- **Nuclear energy** is the huge amount of energy that holds together the nucleus of every single atom.

- **Nuclear energy** fuels atom bombs and power stations – and every star in the Universe. It can be released either by fisson or fusion.

- **Nuclear fusion** is when nuclear energy is released by the joining together of nuclei – as inside stars, where they are squeezed together by gravity, and in hydrogen bombs.

- **Usually only tiny nuclei** such as those of hydrogen and helium fuse (join). Only under extreme pressure in huge, collapsing stars do big nuclei like iron fuse.

- **Nuclear fission** is when nuclear energy is released by the splitting of nuclei. This is the method used in most power stations and in atom bombs.

- **Nuclear fission** involves splitting big nuclei like Uranium-235 and plutonium.

- **When a nucleus splits,** it shoots out gamma rays, neutrons (see atoms) and intense heat.

- **In an atom bomb** the energy is released in one second.

- **In a power station,** control rods make sure nuclear reactions are slowed and energy released gradually.

▲ *Nuclear weapons get their power from the transformation of matter in atoms into energy. Only two nuclear weapons have ever been used, during World War II. The first was dropped on the Japanese city of Hiroshima, killing from 70,000 to 100,000 people and destroying 13 square kilometres of the city. Today's nuclear weapons are up to 40 times as powerful as the Hiroshima bomb.*

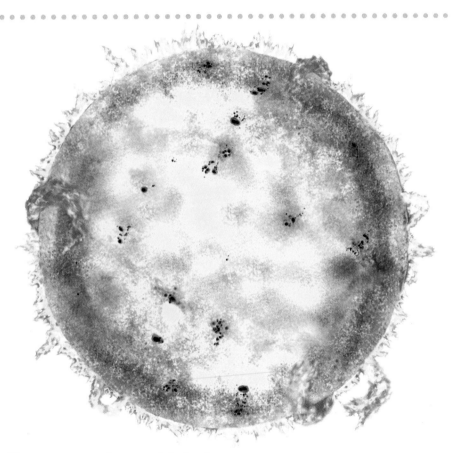

▲ *The temperature at the centre of the Sun is many millions of degrees. This temperature causes the nuclei of atoms to join together in thermonuclear fusion. Through this process the Sun is able to continually radiate enough energy to make life on Earth possible.*

...**FASCINATING FACT**...
The Hiroshima bomb released 84 trillion joules of energy. A supernova releases 125,000 trillion trillion times as much.

Radiation

- **Radiation is energy** shot out at high speed by atoms. There are two main forms – radioactivity and electromagnetic radiation.

- **Radiation either travels** as waves or as tiny particles called photons (see light).

- **Radioactivity is when** an atom decays (breaks down) and sends out deadly energy such as gamma rays.

- **Nuclear radiation** is the radiation from the radioactivity generated by atom bombs and power stations. In large doses, this can cause radiation sickness and death.

- **Electromagnetic radiation** is electric and magnetic fields (see magnetism) that move together in tiny bursts of waves or photons.

- **There are different kinds** of electromagnetic radiation, each one with a different wavelength.

▲ *The Sun throws out huge quantities of radiation of all kinds. Fortunately, our atmosphere protects us from the worst.*

- **Gamma rays** are a very short-wave, energetic and dangerous form of electromagnetic radiation.

- **Radio waves** are a long-wave, low-energy radiation.

- **In between these** come X-rays, ultraviolet rays, visible light, infrared rays and microwaves.

- **Together these forms** of electromagnetic radiation are called the electromagnetic spectrum. Visible light is the only part of the spectrum we can see with our eyes.

- **All electromagnetic rays** move at the speed of light – 300,000 km per second.

- **Everything we detect** in space is picked up by the radiation it gives out (see the Big Bang).

▼ *The electromagnetic spectrum includes a huge range of different energy waves, with different wavelengths and properties. All, however, travel in the same way.*

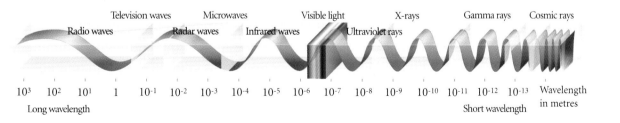

Television waves   Microwaves   Visible light   X-rays   Gamma rays   Cosmic rays

Radio waves   Radar waves   Infrared waves   Ultraviolet rays

10^3 10^2 10^1 1 10^{-1} 10^{-2} 10^{-3} 10^{-4} 10^{-5} 10^{-6} 10^{-7} 10^{-8} 10^{-9} 10^{-10} 10^{-11} 10^{-12} 10^{-13} Wavelength in metres

Long wavelength   Short wavelength

23

Light

- **Light is the fastest thing** in the Universe, travelling at 299,792,458 metres per second.

- **Light rays always travel** in straight lines.

- **Light rays change direction** as they pass from one material to another. This is called refraction.

- **Colours** are different wavelengths of light.

- **The longest light waves** you can see are red, and the shortest are violet.

- **Light is a form** of electromagnetic radiation (see magnetism and radiation), and a light ray is a stream of tiny energy particles called photons.

- **Photons of light** travel in waves just 380 to 750 nanometres (millionths of a millimetre) long.

- **Faint light** from very distant stars is often recorded by sensors called CCDs (see observatories). These count photons from the star as they arrive and build up a picture of the star bit by bit over a long period.

- **The electromagnetic spectrum** (range) includes ultraviolet light and X-rays, but light is the only part of the spectrum our eyes can see.

- **All light is given out by atoms,** and atoms give out light when 'excited' – for example, in a nuclear reaction.

▶ *Light rays passing through transparent substances like water and glass slow down and so appear to bend – refraction. Lenses use this effect to make things look bigger and smaller.*

▲ *Massive nuclear reactions within stars cause them to emit vast amounts of light and other types of radiation.*

Elements

- **Elements** are the basic chemicals of the Universe. There are no simpler substances, and they cannot be broken down into other substances.

- **Elements are formed** entirely of atoms that contain the same number of protons in their nuclei (see atoms). All hydrogen atoms have one proton, for instance.

- **More than 100 elements** are known.

- **The simplest and lightest elements** – hydrogen and helium – formed very early in the history of the Universe (see the Big Bang).

- **Other elements** formed as the nuclei of the atoms of the light elements joined in a process called nuclear fusion.

- **Nuclear fusion of element atoms** happens deep inside stars because of the pressure of their gravity.

- **Lighter elements** like oxygen and carbon formed first.

- **Helium nuclei** fused with oxygen and neon atoms to form atoms like silicon, magnesium and calcium.

- **Heavy atoms** like iron formed when massive supergiant stars neared the end of their life and collapsed, boosting the pressure of the gravity in their core hugely. Even now iron is forming inside dying supergiants.

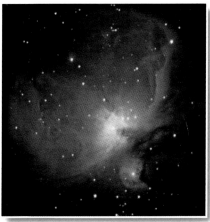

▲ *Nebulae like this one, Orion, contain many elements. Some (such as oxygen, silicon and carbon) formed in their stars, but their hydrogen and helium formed in deep space very long ago.*

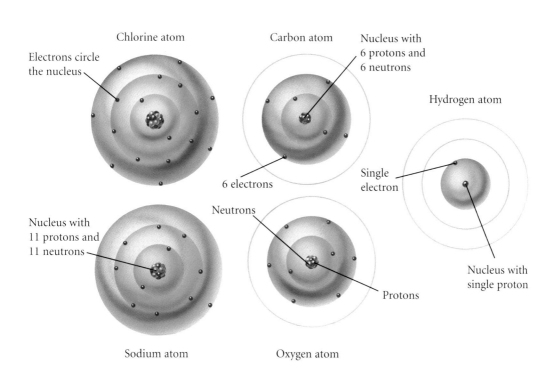

Chlorine atom

Electrons circle
the nucleus

Carbon atom

Nucleus with
6 protons and
6 neutrons

Hydrogen atom

6 electrons

Single
electron

Neutrons

Nucleus with
11 protons and
11 neutrons

Nucleus with
single proton

Protons

Sodium atom

Oxygen atom

▲ All the atoms of an element have the same
number of protons. All atoms except those of
the simplest form of hydrogen also contain
neutrons (particles with no electric charge) in
their nucleus. Electrons have so much energy
that they circle the nucleus at different distances
depending on how much energy they have.

. . . FASCINATING FACT . . .
Massive atoms like uranium and thorium are
formed by the shock waves from supernovae.

Magnetism

- **Magnetism is a force** that either pulls magnetic materials together or pushes them apart.

- **Iron and nickel** are the most common magnetic materials. Electricity is also magnetic.

- **Around every magnet** there is a region in which its effects are felt, called its magnetic field.

- **The magnetic field** around a planet or a star is called the magnetosphere.

- **Most of the planets** in the Solar System, including the Earth, have a magnetic field.

- **Planets have magnetic fields** because of the liquid iron in their cores. As the planets rotate, so the iron swirls, generating electric currents that create the magnetic field.

- **Jupiter's magnetic field** is 30 times stronger than that of the Earth, because Jupiter is huge and spins very quickly.

- **Neptune and Uranus** are unusual because, unlike other planets' magnetic fields, theirs are at right angles to their axis of rotation (the angle at which they spin).

- **Magnetism is linked** to electricity, and together they make up the force called electromagnetism.

- **Electromagnetism** is one of the four fundamental forces in the Universe, along with gravity and the two basic forces of the atomic nucleus.

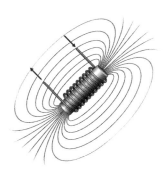

▲ *Electromagnetism is one of the fundamental forces in the Universe. In everyday life electromagnets are essential to power electric motors.*

▲ *The planet Jupiter is one of the most powerful magnets in the Solar System. It was first detected by 'synchrotron radiation' – the radiation from tiny electrons accelerating as they fall into a magnetic field.*

Gravity

- **Gravity** is the attraction, or pulling force, between all matter.

- **Gravity** is what holds everything on Earth on the ground and stops it flying off into space. It holds the Earth together, keeps the Moon orbiting the Earth, and the Earth and all the planets orbiting the Sun.

- **Gravity** makes stars burn by squeezing their matter together.

- **The force of gravity** is the same everywhere.

- **The force of gravity** depends on mass (the amount of matter in an object) and distance.

- **The more mass an object has,** and the closer it is to another object, the more strongly its gravity pulls.

- **Black holes** have the strongest gravitational pull in the entire Universe.

- **The basic laws of gravity** can be used for anything from detecting an invisible planet by studying the flickers in another star's light, to helping the flight of a space probe.

▼ *The* Apollo *astronauts' steps upon the Moon were the first human experience of another space object's gravity.*

● **Einstein's theory of general relativity** shows that gravity not only pulls on matter, but also bends space and even time itself (see Einstein).

● **Orbits are the result** of a perfect balance between the force of gravity on an object (which pulls it inward towards whatever it is orbiting), and its forward momentum (which keeps it flying straight onwards).

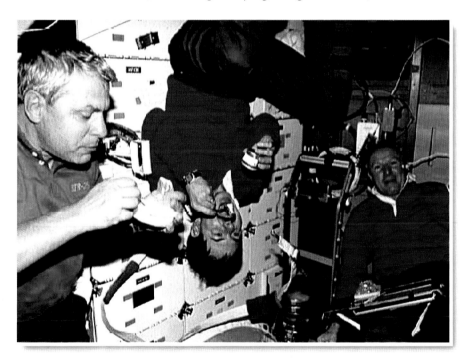

▲ *Lack of gravity in space makes astronauts float around the cabin, unless they are tied onto a fixed object.*

Black holes

- **Black holes** are places where gravity is so strong that it sucks everything in, including light.

- **If you fell** into a black hole you'd stretch like spaghetti.

- **Black holes** form when a star or galaxy gets so dense that it collapses under the pull of its own gravity.

- **Black holes** may exist at the heart of every galaxy.

- **Gravity shrinks** a black hole to an unimaginably small point called a singularity.

- **Around a singularity,** gravity is so intense that space-time is bent into a funnel.

- **Matter spiralling** into a black hole is torn apart and glows so brightly that it creates the brightest objects in the Universe – quasars.

- **The swirling gases** around a black hole turn it into an electrical generator, making it spout jets of electricity billions of kilometres out into space.

- **The opposite of black holes** may be white holes which spray out matter and light like fountains.

▲ *This is an artist's impression of what a black hole might look like, with jets of electricity shooting out from either side.*

▶ *No light is able to escape from a black hole. Scientists know where they are because they affect the light emitted by nearby stars.*

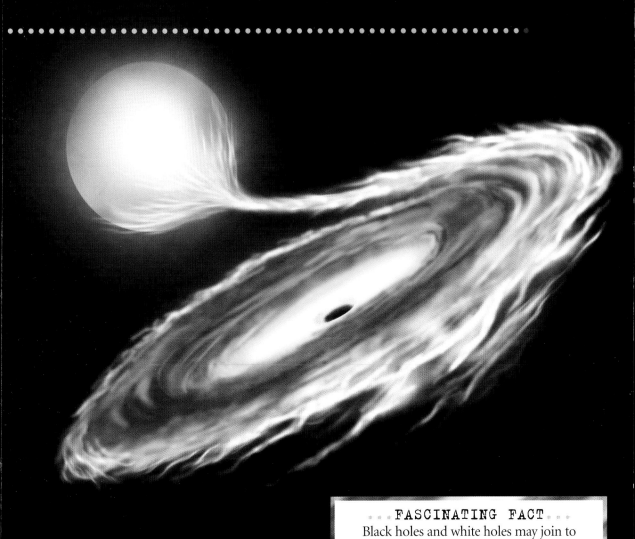

Dark matter

- **Dark matter** is space matter we cannot see because, unlike stars and galaxies, it does not give off light.

- **There is much more dark matter** in the Universe than bright. Some scientists think 90% of matter is dark.

- **Astronomers know about dark matter** because its gravity pulls on stars and galaxies, changing their orbits and the way they rotate (spin round).

- **The visible stars in the Milky Way** are only a thin central slice, embedded in a big bun-shaped ball of dark matter.

- **Dark matter** is of two kinds – the matter in galaxies (galactic), and the matter between them (intergalactic).

- **Galactic dark matter** may be much the same as ordinary matter. However, it burnt out (as black dwarf stars do) early in the life of the Universe.

- **Intergalactic dark matter** is made up of WIMPs (Weakly Interacting Massive Particles).

- **Some WIMPs** are called cold dark matter because they are travelling slowly away from the Big Bang.

- **Some WIMPs** are called hot dark matter because they are travelling very fast away from the Big Bang.

- **The future of the Universe** may depend on how much dark matter there is. If there is too much, its gravity will eventually stop the Universe's expansion – and make it shrink again (see the Big Bang).

▲ *A galaxy's bright stars may be only a tiny part of its total matter. Much of the galaxy may be invisible dark matter.*

▲ *Astronomers determined the amount of dark matter in clusters of galaxies by measuring arcs of light. These arcs occur when the gravity of a cluster bends light from distant galaxies.*

Space telescopes

- **Space telescopes** are launched as satellites so we can study the Universe without interference from Earth's atmosphere.

- **The first space telescope** was Copernicus, sent up in 1972.

- **The most famous** is the Hubble space telescope, launched from a space shuttle in 1990.

- **Different space telescopes** study all the different forms of radiation that make up the electromagnetic spectrum (see light).

- **The COBE satellite** picks up microwave radiation which may be left over from the Big Bang.

- **The IRAS satellite** studied infrared radiation from objects as small as space dust.

- **Space telescopes** that study ultraviolet rays from the stars included the International Ultraviolet Explorer (IUE), launched in 1978.

- **Helios** was one of many space telescopes studying the Sun.

- **X-rays** can only be picked up by space telescopes such as the Einstein, ROSAT and XTE satellites.

- **Gamma rays** can only be picked up by space telescopes like the Compton Gamma-Ray Observatory.

▶ *The Hubble space telescope's main mirror was faulty when it was launched, but a replacement was fitted by shuttle astronauts in 1994.*

37

Space exploration

- **Space is explored** in two ways – by studying it from Earth using powerful telescopes, and by launching spacecraft to get a closer view.

- **Most space exploration** is by unmanned space probes.

- **The first pictures** of the far side of the Moon were sent back by the *Luna 3* space probe in October 1959.

- **Manned missions** have only reached as far as the Moon, but there may be a manned mission to Mars in 2020.

- **Apollo astronauts** took three days to reach the Moon.

- **No space probe** has ever come back from another planet.

- **Travel to the stars** would take hundreds of years, but one idea is that humans might go there inside gigantic spaceships made from hollowed-out asteroids.

- **Another idea is that spacecraft** on long voyages of exploration may be driven along by pulses of laser light.

- **The *Pioneer 10* and *11* probes** carry metal plaques with messages for aliens telling them about us.

▲ Apollo 11, *the US spacecraft that made the famous journey to the Moon, in 1969.*

▲ *Most space exploration is by unmanned probes, guided by on-board computers and equipped with various devices which feed data back to Earth via radio signals.*

...FASCINATING FACT...
NASA may fund research on spacecraft
that jump to the stars through wormholes
(see black holes).

Index